Smart Alec's

CHEEKY JOKES

FATCHOPS
BOT -
MY TEECHER -
<u>SIGNED</u>
THE
PURPUL FANTUM

Smart Alec's

CHEEKY JOKES

for KIDS

ILLUSTRATED BY D. MOSTYN (ALIAS POOR STARVING ARTIST!)

← HENRY BOTS PAD

I'M A NO.9. AN' I'M IN THIS BOOK SO THERE!!

Ward Lock Limited · London

© Ward Lock Limited 1987

First published in Great Britain in 1987
by Ward Lock Limited, 8 Clifford Street
London W1X 1RB, an Egmont Company

Typeset by Columns of Reading
Printed and bound in Great Britain
by Collins

British Library Cataloguing in Publication Data

Smart Alec's cheeky jokes for kids.
  I. Alec, *Smart*
  828'.91402   PZ8.7

  ISBN 0–7063–6609–3

Alec: 'When I grow up I want to be a millionaire. I'll own a big mansion without any bathrooms.'
John: 'Why no bathrooms?'
Alec: 'Because I want to be *filthy* rich!'

Girlfriend: 'I spend hours in front of the mirror admiring my beauty. Do you think it's vanity?'
Alec: 'No — just imagination.'

Mother: 'Did you thank Mrs Smith for inviting you to the party?'
Alec: 'No — the boy before me thanked her and Mrs Smith said, "Don't mention it." So I didn't.'

'How can you make a tall man short?'
　'Ask him to lend you all his money.'

Young sister: 'Is it good manners to eat chicken with your fingers?'
Alec: 'No, you should eat your fingers separately.'

Father: 'How can you claim that a forger is a good person?'
Alec: 'Because he's always writing wrongs!'

'What can a busy gardener always grow?'
   'Tired!'

Woman: 'My child has just fallen down a well. What should I do?'
Alec: 'Buy a book on how to bring up children!'

GETTING WORKED UP

FIRST WE HAD JOKES ABOUT ANIMALS — THEN ALL THAT KNOCK KNOCK STUFF... *

Father: 'There's a new restaurant where we can all eat dirt cheap.'
Alec: 'But who wants to eat dirt?'

Alec: 'Since we met, I can't eat or drink.'
Girlfriend: 'Why not?'
Alec: 'I'm broke!'

Alec: 'I'd like to buy a puppy. How much are they?'
Pet-shop owner: 'Ten pounds apiece.'
Alec: 'And how much does a whole one cost?'

* SEE "SMART ALEC'S BEASTLY JOKES FOR KIDS AND SMART ALEC'S KNOCK KNOCK JOKES FOR KIDS."

WATCH THIS SPACE FANS! YOU'LL SEE SOMETHING HORRIBLE. FLICK THROUGH FROM THE BACK!

Uncle: 'I made two trips across the Atlantic and never took a bath.'
Alec: 'I'd say that makes you a dirty double crosser!'

Alec: 'I met a girl with pedestrian eyes.'
Friend: 'What are pedestrian eyes?'
Alec: 'They look both ways when they cross.'

Mother: 'When Mrs Weatherby gave you an orange, what did you say?'
Alec: 'Peel it!'

I DON'T UNDERSTAND ANY OF IT!

John: 'Why do you call your girlfriend Peach?'
Alec: 'Because she's got a heart of stone.'

Friend: 'I can lie in bed and watch the sun rise.'
Alec: 'So what? I can sit on a stool and watch the kitchen sink!'

Teacher: 'I asked everyone to draw a ring. Why did you draw a square?'
Alec: 'This square is a ring — a *boxing* ring!'

Alec: 'This soup is terrible.'
Waiter: 'Why do you say that?'
Alec: 'A little swallow told me!'

1

Mother: 'I believe I have the face of a twenty-year-old girl.'
Alec: 'Well, you'd better give it back — you're getting it all wrinkled!'

Man: 'I've just crashed my expensive car.'
Alec: 'That's the way the Mercedes Benz!'

'Can you stretch the music out a bit longer?'
   'Sorry, madam, this is a dance band not a rubber band.'

Friend: 'What was SnowWhite's brother's name?'
Alec: 'Egg White. Get the yolk?'

Girlfriend: 'Do you think it's O.K. for me to wear my new fur coat in the rain?'
Alec: 'Have you ever seen a squirrel carrying an umbrella?'

Dentist: 'What kind of filling do you want me to put in your tooth?'
Alec: 'My preference is chocolate fudge!'

'Waiter, what's this fly doing in my soup?'
  'It looks like the backstroke!'

John: 'My uncle changed his will six times this year.'
Alec: 'He's obviously a fresh heir fiend!'

HI FANS — DO YOU LIKE SO FAR?

Aunt: 'When do you like school best?'
Alec: 'When it's closed!'

Girlfriend: 'Did you notice how the opera singer's voice filled the hall?'
Alec: 'Yes. I also noticed that a lot of people left to make room for it!'

Alec: 'A dog just bit me on my ankle.'
Doctor: 'Did you put anything on it?'
Alec: 'No, he liked it just as it was!'

Teacher: 'If I had ten apples in one hand and twelve apples in the other, what would I have?'
Alec: 'The biggest hands anyone's ever seen!'

Landowner: 'You're not allowed to fish here.'
Alec: 'I'm not fishing, I'm giving my pet worm a bath!'

Girlfriend: 'Did your watch stop when you dropped it on the floor?'
Alec: 'Of course! Did you think it would go right through the ground?'

Friend: 'So your father collects fleas. What does your mother do?'
Alec: 'Scratch!'

WORM SOAP

Teacher: 'What's the definition of a cannibal?'
Alec: 'Someone who's fed up with people.'

'Why are you about to set fire to that jacket?'
   'Dad said it was a blazer!'

Alec: 'A girlfriend of mine went on a coconut diet.'
John: 'How much weight did she lose?'
Alec: 'None, but you should see her climb trees!'

'Doctor, doctor, my son has just swallowed a bullet. What should I do?'
   'To begin with, don't point him at me!'

John: 'My father can play the piano by ear.'
Alec: 'So what? My father can fiddle with his whiskers!'

Alec: 'What does the X-ray of my brain show?'
Doctor: 'Nothing.'

Girlfriend: 'I've just swallowed a roll of film.'
Alec: 'Not to worry, nothing serious can develop.'

RIPPLING ARPEGGIOS

John: 'The ointment the doctor gave me makes my hands smart.'
Alec: 'Then I suggest you rub some on your head.'

Friend: 'Where do fleas go in winter?'
Alec: 'Search me!'

Music teacher: 'Can you sing tenor?'
Alec: 'I would if I could but I don't know the words.'

Mother: 'Wash your hands, your piano teacher will soon be here.'
Alec: 'Don't worry, I'll only play on the black notes!'

Teacher: 'Why are the Middle Ages called the Dark Ages?'
Alec: 'That's easy — because there were so many knights in them!'

'How did the blind carpenter regain his sight?'
   'He picked up a hammer and saw!'

'What do you mean you're going to be a robber? That's dangerous!'
   'Not really. I'm going to be a *safe* robber!'

THAT IS CHEEKY!!

Alec: 'I want to buy a chicken for my mother.'
Butcher: 'Do you want a pullet?'
Alec: 'No, I'll carry it home!'

'Why are you cleaning up the spilled soup with your cake?'
    'It's a sponge cake!'

Mother: 'The florist has two children.'
Alec: 'I know, one is a budding genius and the other is a blooming idiot!'

Doctor: 'How did you get here so fast?'
Alec: 'Flu!'

'*What happened to the couple who met in a revolving door?*'
   'They're still going around together!'

Alec: 'I can lift an elephant with one hand.'
Friend: 'That's impossible.'
Alec: 'No it's not. Find me an elephant with one hand and I'll prove it to you!'

Mother: 'How did you get that swelling on your nose?'
Alec: 'I bent down to smell a brose.'
Mother: 'It's not brose, it's rose. There's no B in rose.'
Alec: 'There was in this one!'

'*Waiter, will my hamburger be long?*'
   'No, sir, it will be round.'

DID I HEAR HAMBURGER?

Alec: 'Did you hear the story about the three eggs?'
Friend: 'No.'
Alec: 'Two bad.'

Girlfriend: 'Now we've decided to get engaged, I hope you'll give me a ring.'
Alec: 'Of course I will. What's your number?'

'You say your girlfriend fell overboard in shark-infested waters but the sharks didn't bother her?'
   'That's right. They were man-eating sharks.'

Mother: 'Did you give the goldfish fresh water?'
Alec: 'No, they haven't drunk what I gave them yesterday.'

Teacher: 'Spell mouse.'
Alec: 'M-O-U-S.'
Teacher: 'But what's on the end of it?'
Alec: 'A tail!'

'Where was Queen Victoria going when she was in her 39th year?'
  'Into her 40th!'

Sister: 'I heard a loud noise this morning.'
Alec: 'It must have been the crack of dawn!'

Alec: 'When I go to a restaurant, I think of the cutlery as a form of medicine.'
Friend: 'How do you mean?'
Alec: 'To be taken after meals!'

'Doctor, doctor, I have a terrible problem. Can you help me out?'
   'Certainly. Which way did you come in?'

Alec: 'Are waiters supposed to be tipped?'
Waiter: 'Of course.'
Alec: 'Good, then tip me. I've been waiting for service for twenty minutes!'

Teacher: 'On what did the ancient Gauls inscribe their records?'
Alec: 'Gallstones.'

Teacher: 'What is a prickly pear?'
Alec: 'Two porcupines.'

Teacher: 'Where was the Magna Carta signed?'
Alec: 'At the bottom. Where else?'

'Why do you say that Rome must have been built at night?'
  'I keep hearing people say it wasn't built in a day!'

Teacher: 'Where are the kings and queens of Great Britain usually crowned?'
Alec: 'On the head, of course!'

Teacher: 'The ruler of Russia was called the Czar and his wife was the Czarina. What were their children called?'
Alec: 'Czardines!'

'What did Caesar say when Brutus stabbed him?'
    'OUCH!'

Teacher: 'We all know a comet is a star with a tail. Name one.'
Alec: 'Lassie!'

Teacher: 'Why does the Statue of Liberty stand in New York Harbour?'
Alec: 'Because it can't sit down!'

'In the alphabet, what comes after O?'
  'Yeah!'

Mother: 'You've put your shoes on the wrong feet.'
Alec: 'But these are the only feet I have!'

Mother: 'Why did you put this live frog in your sister's bed?'
Alec: 'Because I couldn't find a dead mouse!'

'*We had to have our dog put down.*'
  'Was it mad?'
'*Well, it wasn't exactly happy!*'

'*How many people work in your office?*'
  'About half of them.'

'*Why are you scratching yourself?*'
  'Because nobody else knows exactly where I itch!'

Waiter: 'How did you find your steak, sir?'
Alec: 'I looked under a chip, and there it was!'

'I can't seem to fall asleep at night.'
   "Try sleeping by the edge of the bed. You'll
   soon drop off!'

Dad: 'How were the exam questions?'
Alec: 'Fine. It was the answers I had trouble
with!'

Teacher: 'What month has 28 days?'
Alec: 'All of them!'

Teacher: 'How can you prove the world is round?'
Alec: 'I never claimed it was, sir.'

Captain: 'Why didn't you bother to stop the ball, then?'
Goalie: 'I figure that's what the net's for!'

Vicar: 'You shouldn't fight, you should learn to give and take.'
Alec: 'I did. I gave him a black eye and took his apple.'

Alec: 'Would you punish a kid for something he didn't do?'
Teacher: 'Of course not.'
Alec: 'Good. I didn't do my homework!'

'Waiter, there's a dead fly in my soup.'
   'Yes, it's the heat that kills them!'

Teacher: 'How fast does light travel?'
Alec: 'I'm not sure, but I do know it always gets here too early in the morning!'

'Did you know that deep breathing kills germs?'
   'Really? How do you get them to breathe deeply?'

Nurse: 'You seem to be coughing more easily this morning.'
Alec: 'And why not? I've been practising all night!'

Alec: 'I'm tired.'
Father: 'You're lazy. Hard work never killed anyone.'
Alec: 'I don't want to run the risk of being the first!'

Teacher: 'Spell elephant.'
Alec: 'E-L-E-F-A-N-T.'
Teacher: 'The dictionary spells it E-L-E-P-H-A-N-T.'
Alec: 'You asked me how *I* spelt it, not how the dictionary spelt it!'

Friend: 'Is it really bad luck to have a black cat follow you?'
Alec: 'It all depends whether you're a man or a mouse!'

Father: 'Why did you sleep under the car?'
Alec: 'I wanted to get up oily in the morning!'

'Would you like a pocket calculator for Christmas?'
   'Not really. I already know how many pockets I have.'

'Does this band take requests?'
   'Certainly.'
'Good. I request they stop playing!'

'My baby is a year old today, and he's been walking since he was nine months old.'
   'Really? He must be very tired!'

Judge: 'Haven't you been up before me before?'
Prisoner: 'I'm not sure. What time do you get up?'

Alec: 'Do you have a good memory for faces?'
Father: 'Yes, why?'
Alec: 'I've just broken your shaving mirror!'

Teacher: 'Name the four seasons.'
Alec: 'Pepper, salt, vinegar and mustard.'

Sergeant: 'What were you before you joined the army?'
New recruit: 'Happy!'

Teacher: 'If you found 25p in one pocket and 40p in another pocket, what would you have?'
Alec: 'Somebody else's trousers!'

Alec: 'There's one motorist who's never troubled by back-seat drivers.'
Friend: 'Who's that?'
Alec: 'The man who drives a hearse!'

Teacher: 'What's the difference between a porpoise and a dolphin?'
Alec: 'That's what I say — what's the difference!'

Alec: 'Dad just bought a baby car.'
Friend: 'What do you mean?'
Alec: 'It won't go anywhere without a rattle.'

Alec: 'Do you have holes in your trousers?'
John: 'Of course not.'
Alec: 'Really. Then how do you get your legs through?'

Alec: 'Every day my dog and I go for a tramp in the woods.'
Friend: 'Does your dog enjoy it?'
Alec: 'Oh yes, but the tramp is a bit fed up!'

Mother: 'Why do you eat everything with your knife?'
Alec: 'My fork leaks!'

Alec: 'When my fingers heal, will I be able to play the piano?'
Doctor: 'Of course.'
Alec: 'Great! I never could before!'

'Have you read the Bible?'
  'No, I'm waiting to see the film!'

Teacher: 'Why were the Red Indians the first people in North America?'
Alec: 'Because they had reservations!'

'He shot a leopard right on the spot.'
  'Which spot?'

Teacher: 'To what family does the rhinoceros belong?'
Alec: 'I don't know, but I'm sure it's no family in our street!'

Mrs Blimp: 'One of my relatives died at Waterloo.'
Alec: 'Really? Which platform?'

'Is your horse well-behaved?'
  'Yes. When we come to a fence he stops and lets me go over first!'

Husband: 'What would you like for Christmas?'
Wife: 'Make it a surprise.'
Husband: 'Right. BOO!'

'Do you like painting people in the nude?'
  'No, I always keep my clothes on!'

Teacher: 'How many fingers have you?'
Alec: 'Ten.'
Teacher: 'And if you lost three of them in an accident, what would you have?'
Alec: 'No more piano lessons!'

Uncle: 'What are you going to give your sister this year for Christmas?'
Alec: 'I'm not sure. Last year I gave her measles!'

Alec: 'Do you believe in free speech?'
Neighbour: 'Of course.'
Alec: 'Good. I need to borrow your phone to make a long-distance call.'

Friend: 'How's your sister getting on with her diet?'
Alec: 'Great. She's almost disappeared!'

'I cured my son of biting his nails.'
  'How did you manage that?'
'I knocked out all his teeth!'

'I suppose this horrible picture is what you call modern art?'
  'No, it's a mirror!'

'Why is your brother crying?'
  'Because I won't give him my piece of
  cake.'
'What about his own piece of cake?'
  'He cried when I ate that too!'

'How can I be certain the trains are running on
time?'
  'Just before the next one arrives put your
  watch on the rail!'

'*I've come to ask for your daughter's hand.*'
   'You'll have to take all of her or there's no deal!'

Friend: 'How do you keep fish from smelling?'
Alec: 'Cut off their noses!'

Friend: 'The police are looking for a man with one eye called Sam.'
Alec: 'What's his other eye called?'

Judge: 'Order, order in the courtroom.'
Alec: 'I'll have some fish and chips with pickles and ice cream!'

* SEE "SMART ALEC'S KNOCK KNOCK JOKES FOR KIDS. IT'S A KNOCK-OUT - HA! HA!

Vicar: 'Do you say a prayer before dinner?'
Alec: 'There's no need. My mum is a good cook!'

'What's the weather like?'
  'I don't know, it's too cloudy to see!'

'Why did you push your friend under a steamroller?'
  'I wanted a flatmate!'

Angry man: 'I'll teach you to throw stones at my greenhouse.'
Alec: 'I wish you would. I keep missing it!'

'I didn't come here to be insulted.'
  'Where do you usually go?'

'Doctor, can you give me something for my liver?'
  'How about some onions?'

'Why does your father work at the bakery?'
  'He kneads the dough!'

Alec told his friend, 'If you want a free headstone when you die, have them bury you up to your neck!'

'There are times when I really like you.'
  'When is that?'
When you're not yourself!'

Alec said to Ivan, 'You're my friend and I'd like to pay you a compliment, but I can't think of one.'

Alec: 'I'm glad you don't have a dual personality.'
Sheila: 'Why?'
Alec: 'The one you have is bad enough!'

John: 'Did you hear the latest joke about dustmen?'
Alec: 'Don't bother to tell it, it's probably just a load of rubbish!'

John: 'I'd like to be a litter collector. Do you think I need some special training?'
Alec: 'Not really, you'll just pick it up as you go along.'

Ivan: 'Why do some women put their hair in rollers before they go to sleep?'
Alec: 'So they'll wake up *curly* in the morning.'

Alec: 'Will this bus take me to Knightsbridge?'
Conductor: 'Which part?'
Alec: 'All of me, of course!'

Wanda: 'How do you like me?'
Alec: 'As girls go, you're fine. And the sooner you go, the better!'

'I keep talking to myself.'
  'No wonder. No one else would listen to you!'

Alec told Harry, 'Your brain is the weakest part of your body, but at least it's protected by the strongest part — your thick skull.'

'How do you find my breath?'
  'Offensive — it's keeping you alive!'

Friend: 'Girls fall in love with me at first sight.'
Alec: 'I know, it's when they take a second look that they can't stand you!'

'Every time I pass a girl she sighs.'
  'With relief!'

'Craig is good at everything he does.'
  'Yes, and as far as I can see he usually does nothing!'

Trudy: 'I was selected by a computer as an ideal girlfriend.'
Alec: 'Who wants to be a computer's girlfriend?'

Alec: 'Did you hear the joke about the rope?'
Andrea: 'No.'
Alec: 'Skip it!'

A bachelor is a wise man. After all, he's never miss-taken!

Certain members of an orchestra can never be trusted — the fiddlers!

'What's the best way to keep water out of the house?'
   'Don't pay your water rates!'

Alec: 'Do you know what the Eskimo girl did to her boyfriend?'
John: 'What?'
Alec: 'She gave him the cold shoulder!'

'There's a twig in my soup.'
   'Call the branch manager!'

'Girls whisper that they love me.'
   'Of course. They'd never admit it out loud!'

'John,' said Alec, 'I have to give you credit. I'd certainly never think of giving you cash!'

'Don't I look distinguished, Alec?'
  'You'll look more distinguished when you're extinguished!'

Carol: 'I want to fight air pollution.'
Alec: 'You could start by not breathing.'

Alec's friend has stopped talking. He's fighting ear pollution!

Paul: 'I have a clear mind.'
Alec: 'You mean, it's not cluttered up with facts.'

Myra: 'What do you think of my musical talent?'
Alec: 'In your case the song should go, "I've got *no* business in show business . . ." '

'This comedian is too dumb to be amusing. I'd say he couldn't even entertain a thought.'

'I'm going to mend my evil ways.'
   'You keep saying that but the stitches are always breaking!'

Joel: 'I feel I'm going to live a long time.'
Alec: 'They say a *cad* has nine lives.'

'I'm sure I'm right.'
   'You're as right as rain — in other words,
   all wet!'

Gwen: 'Harry would never hurt a fly.'
Alec: 'True, he prefers humans.'

'I do lots of exercise.'
   'I can tell. You're certainly long-winded!'

'We should take her at face value.'
   'With a face like hers, that's not worth much!'

'It would take ten men to fill my shoes.'
   'It looks as though it took ten cows to make them!'

Little sister: 'Who do you think invented spaghetti?'
Alec: 'Someone who used his noodle!'

'How do fishermen make their nets?'
  'They take lots of holes and join them
  together!'

'In what country do people always want to
eat?'
  'Hungary!'

Ivan: 'What do you call a butcher's boy?'
Alec: 'A chop assistant!'

'What did the knight in armour say when the
king gave him a medal?'
  'You can't pin that on me.'

BOY - THIS IS SOME
BOOK - HE INSULTS ALL
THE GIRLS THEN HE
BRINGS IN A LOUSY
CAT!

MUTTER
GRUMBLE!!

'What did the Lone Ranger say at the end of his ride?'
   'Whoa!'

Mother: 'Shall I put the kettle on?'
Alec: 'Don't bother; I like the dress you're wearing better!'

Sandra: 'Don't I look lovely today?'
Alec: 'I agree, it's a treat for people to see you. After all, it costs money to get into a freak show!'

'Will you say something good about me at my funeral?'
   'Yes, I'll say you're dead!'

Barry: 'Why are you giving me all this rope?'
Alec: 'They say if you give someone enough rope they'll hang themselves!'

Sister: 'What's the meaning of "opaque"?'
Alec: 'Something through which light can't pass — for example, your skull!'

'His head was so thick, when he joined the army they told him he didn't need to wear a helmet!'

EVERYONE'S GOT TO BE SOMEWHERE

Alec told his friend: 'You should have seen Bernie's wife holding the fish he caught. The scales measured 300 pounds — not counting the fish!'

Neighbour: 'How did you like the food?'
Alec: 'It was a real *swill* dinner!'

'I want a double portion of chips.'
   'Isn't that expensive?'
'No, but it's expansive!'

'The meal was like a good man — I don't think I'm going to be able to keep it down!'

'I've eaten at your house once and all I can say is that meal gave food for thought. It certainly wasn't fit for eating!'

Florence: 'They say two heads are better than one.'
Alec: 'In your case, none is better than one!'

Gail: 'Does your mother have an automatic dishwasher?'
Alec: 'Yes, my father.'

Gail: 'Is your dad henpecked?'
Alec: 'He's so henpecked he bought my mum an automatic dishthrower!'

ALEC'S MUM – OR IS IT HIS DAD?

'*Do you like your mother?*'
   'I can't complain. I don't dare!'

'I don't know how you could ever love a woman who was stupid enough to have married you!'

'I always like to think the best of people. That's why I think of you as an imbecile!'

Barbara: 'Trudy is not very smart. I don't think she'll ever get a job.'
Alec: 'She could always be a ventriloquist's dummy.'

'*Melinda is not a simple person. She has great depth.*'
  'You mean, depth of ignorance.'

'*Do you have trouble making decisions?*'
  'Yes and no!'

'*I wonder what my I.Q. is.*'
  'Don't worry about it, it's nothing.'

'Don't you think I'm funny?'
 'When I listen to you, I realize that humour
 is a serious business.'

'My dad wants to work badly — and he
usually does.'

'He believes in the conservation of energy. He
conserves all he can.'

'My mum wanted a man she could lean on.'
 'My mum did better. She got a man she
 could walk on!'

'What a crybaby!'
  'Yes, he's a regular Prince of Wails!'

'What's the best cure for water on the brain?'
  'A tap on the head!'

Sue: 'How do you keep an idiot waiting?'
Alec: 'I'll tell you tomorrow!'

Alec told his friend, 'My sister is like the jungle — dense!'

Friend: 'My father just bought me a wooden engine with wooden wheels.'
Alec: 'No doubt it wooden go!'

Little sister: 'Why do cows wear bells?'
Alec: 'Because their horns don't work!'

Friend: 'Why do you call your dog Carpenter?'
Alec: 'Because he's always doing little odd jobs around the house!'

John: 'I've heard that Alaskan dogs can run the fastest.'
Alec: 'It's because the trees are so far apart!'

THAT'S WHY I DON'T LIVE IN ALASKA!

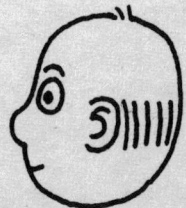

'*Brenda certainly talks a lot.*'
   'I'll say — someone should put a sign on her mouth — OPEN ALL HOURS!'

'She's always talking with her mouth full — of words!'

'*He said he heard it straight from the horse's mouth.*'
   'I know. His dad told him.'

'It's hard for him to eat.'
  'Why?'
'He hates to stop talking.'

*'When he's talking, I always think of an
explosion in a coal mine.'*
  'Why?'
'A lot of noise coming out of a big hole.'

Bob: 'I hear your brother has a quick mind.'
Alec: 'Yes, a real *scheme* engine.'

'It's been so long since he stood upright, his
shadow is crooked!'

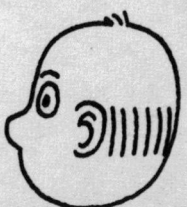

John: 'When I go into the grocer, the shopkeeper always shakes my hand.'
Alec: 'He's hoping to keep it out of the cash register.'

'My brother is very superstitious. In a boxing match he always keeps a horseshoe in his glove.'

'He's hoping for a lucky stroke — for his rich uncle!'

Sheila: 'Is your brother willing to do an honest day's work?'
Alec: 'Yes, but he wants an honest week's pay for it.'

'My brother has a wonderful way of saving money. He forgets whom he borrowed it from.'

'When I lent him money he said, "I'll be everlastingly in your debt." And he was right.'

'My brother fell in love with his wife the second time he saw her. The first time he didn't know she was rich.'

Girlfriend: 'Did he really marry her because her father left her a fortune?'
Alec: 'He denies it. He insists he would have married her no matter who left her a fortune.'

'My brother is so crooked he has to screw his socks on!'

'He's the most highly suspected man in the community.'

'His wallet is always full of big bills — all unpaid!'

* SEE "SMART ALEC'S KNOCK KNOCK - AND BEASTLY JOKES FOR KIDS"

BETTER JOKE
BY STARVING ARTIST

"MY MUM HAD SO MANY CANDLES ON HER BIRTHDAY CAKE WE WERE DRIVEN BACK BY THE HEAT"

HA HA HA !!!

Friend: 'Is your mother one of those women who lie about her age?'
Alec: 'Not really. She says she's as old as dad, then lies about his age!'

'Mum says no more candles on her birthday cake. On her last birthday, there were so many candles it looked like a forest fire!'

'Mum is a very decisive person. When she reached 45 she definitely decided what she wanted to be — 29!'

'Your dad claims to be around 35.'
   'Yes, but he's been around it a few times.'

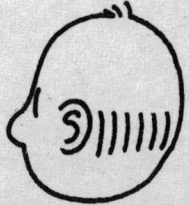

'And my sister isn't lying when she claims she turned 23. She did, ten years ago!'

'How old do you think your neighbour is?'
    'Well, his grandfather was called Adam . . .'

'Your uncle sure drinks a lot.'
    'He sure does — if he keeps going *liquor mortis* will soon set in.'

'It's not true that my uncle does nothing but drink beer. He also hiccups!'

REEK!
HONK!!

'The doctor says Grandad has too little blood in his alcohol system.'

'When he gets a cold he buys a bottle of whisky and in no time it's gone.'
    'The cold or the whisky?'

'He's really the nicest man on two feet — if only he could stay there.'

'When the doctor warned him that alcohol is a slow poison, he answered, "That's O.K., I'm in no hurry." '

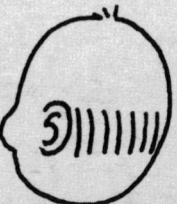

'My uncle believes in a balanced diet. He always keeps a bottle of beer in each hand.'

'In hospital my uncle kept asking for a glass of water. That's how the nurses knew he was going out of his mind.'

Friend: 'I work for your brother and I admire him.'
Alec: 'Of course you do. If you didn't you'd be fired.'

'When he loses to me in tennis, he always grips my hand and shakes it.'
   'Yes, but he wishes it was your throat!'

Friend: 'Your brother says he can lick any man with one hand.'
Alec: 'Perhaps, but he can't get them to fight with one hand.'

'How does your father handle temptation?'
   'He yields to it.'

Friend: 'Is your father brave?'
Alec: 'Brave? When he goes to the doctor he needs an anaesthetic to sit in the waiting room!'

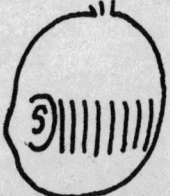

'He bites his nails so much his stomach needs a manicure!'

Friend: 'Is your father a member of the golf club?'
Alec: 'No, he would never join any club that would take someone like him as a member.'

'My mum's hand shakes so much she can thread the needle of a sewing machine when it's running!'

'My brother is as spineless as cooked spaghetti!'

Friend: 'Is it true that your friend Jim is a miracle worker?'
Alec: 'That's correct. It's a miracle when he works!'

'My brother is not very popular in the office. The other workers complain that his snoring disturbs them.'

'Is he really that lazy?'
  'He's so lazy that he sticks his nose out the window so the wind can blow it for him.'

'There's only one job that he'd really like — tester in a mattress factory.'

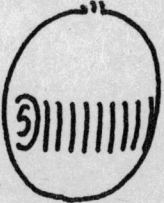

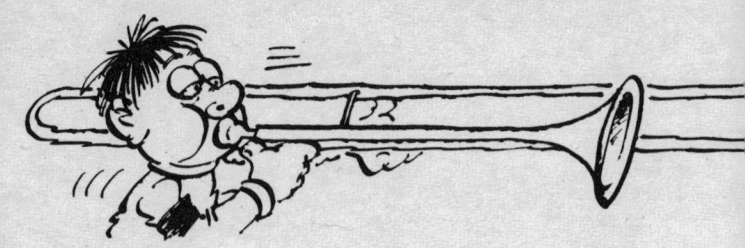

'*Why do you think he decided to learn the trombone?*'
   'It's the only instrument on which you can get anywhere by letting things slide!'

'At bedtime he has his prayers printed and pasted on the wall because he's too lazy to say them. He just says, "Lord, please read them." '

'There's one thing you can say for my brother, he puts in a good day's work. It takes him a month though.'

'He works eight hours and sleeps eight hours. He's being fired because they're the same eight hours.'

Friend: 'Your brother does look tired.'
Alec: 'I agree. I demanded to see his birth certificate to prove that he's alive!'

'He gets his exercise watching horror movies on TV. They make his flesh creep!'

'Doesn't Bill look tired?'
　'Yes. Last week he fell asleep while running for a bus!'

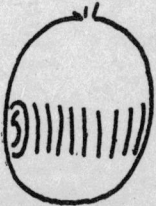

'What did your dad say to your mum when he married her?'
    'He said that a marriage and a career don't mix. Since then he's never worked.'

'How does your sister look in her new bathing suit?'
    'She looks like a real lady — Lady Godiva!'

'My mum's hat is very becoming.'
    'You mean it's becoming worn out!'

'The dresses she wears never go out of style. They look just as ridiculous year after year.'

'*Did you notice the strange growth on my kid brother's neck?*'
   'Yes, it's called his head!'

'Your kid brother is so dumb that when he went to a mind reader he was only charged half price!'

'*Everyone in our family is hoping Tom will get ahead.*'
   'Yes, he looks funny with nothing on the top of his neck.'

'*I'd say your brother has a chip on his shoulder.*'
   'It's probably from the wooden block above.'

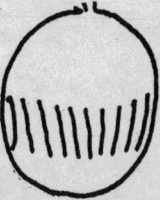

I CAN SMELL SOMETHING!

'*He claims he has a mind of his own.*'
'Of course he does. No one else would want it.'

Alec: 'I've invented a new kind of coffin that just covers the head.'
Friend: 'What's the good of it?'
Alec: 'It's for people like you — dead from the neck up!'

'I feel sorry for your poor little mind, all alone in that great big head!'

'Many doctors have examined his head — but they can't find anything in it.'

'He could go into headhunters' country without fear. They'd have no interest in him.'

'*My mother is beautiful.*'
  'Yes, like a Greek statue — beautiful, but not all there.'

'*My sister's boyfriend calls her baby-face.*'
  'Does he tell her she has a brain to match?'

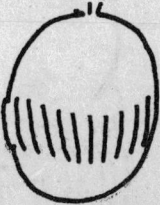

Alec: 'Your brother should be a boxer.'
Friend: 'Why?'
Alec: 'Someone might knock him conscious.'

Friend: 'My brother often has something on his mind.'
Alec: 'Only when he wears a hat.'

'He should be careful not to let his mind wander. It's too weak to be let out alone!'

'When he was promoted from kindergarten he was so excited he cut himself shaving.'

'But he got 100 on his exams.'
   'Yes, 25 in maths, 25 in spelling, 25 in history and 25 in geography.'

'I can't understand why the kids nicknamed him "Corn".'
   'It's because he's always at the foot of the class.'

'They say that ignorance is bliss.'
   'Then you should be the happiest girl in the world!'

Friend: 'What makes you think my sister is stupid?'
Alec: 'She told me she was working on a new invention — colour radio.'

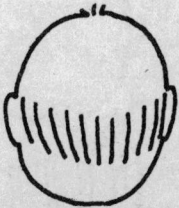

'Why is she standing on her head?'
    'She's turning things over in her mind.'

Friend's sister: 'I want to lose ten pounds of surplus fat.'
Alec: 'Try cutting off your head.'

'My sister won't go swimming in a concrete swimming pool.'
    'Why not?'
'She doesn't like to swim in concrete.'

'My brother stopped a man from beating a donkey.'
    'Really? It must have been a case of brotherly love!'

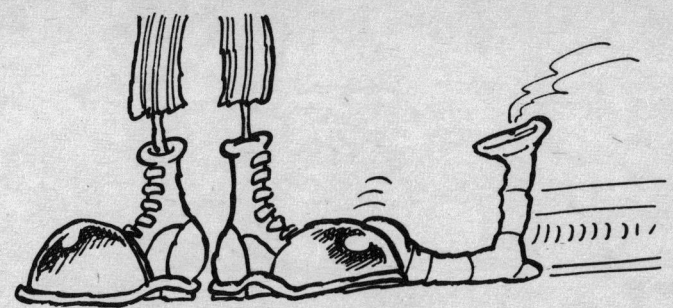

'My dad never takes off his boots.'
'He's probably afraid he'll hurt his toes when he kicks the bucket!'

Friend: 'My mum lies in the sun for hours and hours.'
Alec: 'No doubt she wants to be the toast of the town.'

Alec: 'There's no point in telling you a joke with a double meaning.'
Friend: 'Why not?.'
Alec: 'You won't get either of them.'

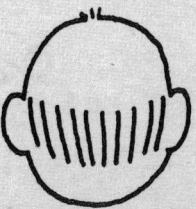

'He probably couldn't spell OTTO backwards!'

Friend: 'I just read that a woman gives birth to a baby every minute.'
Alec: 'Someone should find her and stop her!'

'I want to live to 110.'
    'I know why. Very few people die after that age.'

'More people die in bed than anywhere else.'
    'In that case don't ever go to sleep and you'll live for ever.'

'Someone gave my dad an electric toothbrush, but he won't use it because he can't figure out if his teeth are AC or DC!'

'My brother is finding it hard to find a wife. He's looking for a woman who will love him as much as he does!'

'She can't see any further than the nose on her face.'
　'With her nose that's quite a distance.'

'I want you to accept my opinion for what it's worth.'
    'In that case you owe me 2p.'

Eric: 'That new kid Johnny really has staying power.'
Alec: 'I know. He never leaves!'

'My dad is welcome in the best homes.'
    'Of course he is. He's a plumber!'

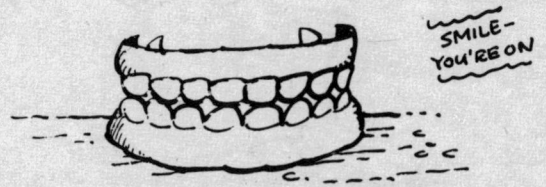

SMILE— YOU'RE ON

'He's not a very sincere person. In fact, the only genuine thing about him is his false teeth!'

'My brother's been at university for many years.'
   'I know — I hear he has more degrees than a thermometer.'

Jean: 'Look at me! Don't I have a perfect shape?'
Alec: 'Perfectly round!'

'Is your stomach O.K.?'
   'Why do you ask?'
'I just wanted to know if it was as sour as your face.'

'*Dad keeps saying that Mum is very dear to him.*'
   'He means she costs him a fortune!'

'*What do you mean "Plan Ahead?"* '
   'Look in the mirror. The one you have now is a mess.'

'*Your dad's a weakling.*'
   'Not nearly as weak as your dad. The only thing he ever licked was people's boots!'

'*You're only as old as you think.*'
   'In that case you must be about three months.'

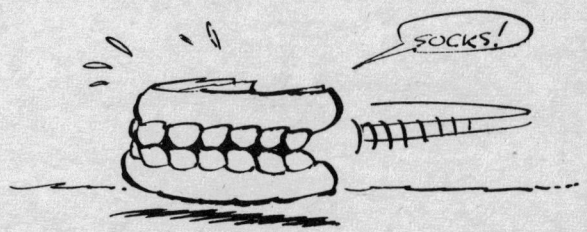

'*I never act stupid.*'
   No. With you it's always the real thing.'

'*My grandparents are real swingers.*'
   'From tree to tree?'

'Let's have an agreement: if you don't say anything, I won't listen.'

'*His thoughts are written all over his face.*'
   'Yes, he certainly has a blank expression.'

'I'm thinking hard.'
  'Don't you mean it's hard for you to think?'

'I should be elevated above all others.'
  'By your neck!'

'Go to your barber to get a haircut. Come to me for your throat.'

'My wife has gone to the beauty parlour.'
  'I didn't know they could perform miracles!'

'*Do you think she looks bad?*'
  'She could look worse — if I had better eyesight.'

Neighbour: 'My son plays the violin, he's had many requests.'
Alec: 'So I understand, but he insists on playing anyway.'

'Music has a horrible effect upon her. It makes her sing!'

George: 'My girlfriend's as pretty as a flower.'
Alec: 'A cauliflower?'

'I don't want to say she's not pretty. Let's just say if you pulled her pigtail she would probably say, "Oink, oink!" '

'I told my husband to tell me everything he knows.'
'He must have been speechless.'

George: 'I think faster than you.'
Alec: 'I can tell. You've stopped already.'

I'VE BEEN CROSSED IN LOVE

THAT SMART
ALEC'S SO
SMART—

'Let's play a game of wits.'
  'No, let's choose a game you can play too!'

Louis: 'I have a ready wit.'
Alec: 'Let me know when it's ready.'

'Does your husband have a happy home life?'
  'It's hard to tell. He's never there.'

'My wife had our house built in a canyon with
an echo. Now she can listen to herself talk
without even speaking.'

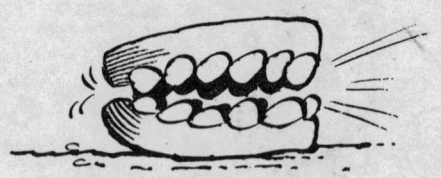

'I've been told I have an infectious smile.'
  'In that case, don't stand too close to me.'

'Men say I'm one in a million.'
  'Thank heavens.'

'Words fail me.'
  'That's because of the way you use them.'

'No one works as effortlessly as my dad. He never lifts a finger.'

Friend: 'My mum's gone on a crash diet.
Alec: 'I can tell. She certainly looks like a wreck!'

'Sir Edwin is a man of breeding.'
  'I know. He's got loads of kids.'

Hal: 'That new kid is a real pain.'
Alec: 'He could be worse. He could be a twin!'

*'Look at my new baby brother. The stork
brought him.'*
   'He looks more like a seagull dropped him.'

Carol: 'I like nightlife . . .'
Alec: 'Owls, rodents . . .'

Alec: 'You'd make a perfect —'
Carol: 'Perfect what?'
Alec: 'Stranger!'

'My father helps the church a great deal.'
   'So I understand. He never goes inside it!'

'O.K., wise guy, you've got blue
eyes — how would you like black ones?'

'My mum is always looking in the mirror.'
  'Not when she's backing out of a parking
  space!'

*'My mum has never said an unkind thing about
anyone.'*
  'That's because she only talks about herself.'

'My dad is happy we live in the machine age.'
  'That's because he thinks he's a big wheel.'

Geraldine: 'My father suffers from migraine.'
Alec: 'That's probably because his halo is too tight.'

'Do you think he's conceited?'
  'Who else has a mirror on the bathroom ceiling so he can watch himself gargle?'

'He's a real big gun in the office.'
  'He should be careful or they might fire him.'

'I tell you he's not conceited.'
   'No, he just loves his good looks and personality.'

'I've often wondered why he never takes a shower.'
   'It's probably because the steam clouds the mirror so he can't admire himself!'

Len: 'Your sister seems very shy.'
Alec: 'I'll say. She covers the bird cage when she undresses!'

'Just look at him. Isn't he a seedy character?'
   'Seedy! Why, he trembles every time he passes a canary!'

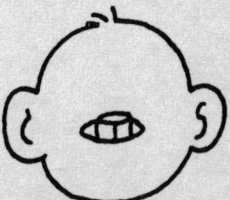

'My boss was sorry when I told him I was quitting next week.'
    'He was probably hoping it was this week.'

'I've been staying awake nights trying to figure out how to succeed.'
    'You might be better off staying awake during the day.'

'I'm now going steady with a girl who's different from the other girls.'
    'You bet she's different. She's the only girl in town who'll go out with you.'

'Jane has very keen senses.'
    'Yes, but there's one sense she hasn't got — *common sense!*'

'Nobody can call her a quitter.'
   'Of course not. She's been fired from every job she's had.'

'My dad started at the bottom, and he enjoyed it so much he's stayed there ever since.'

'Whenever opportunity knocks he probably complains about the noise.'

Lenny: 'My dad took an aptitude test to find out what he was best suited for.'
Alec: 'I know. They discovered he was best suited for retirement.'

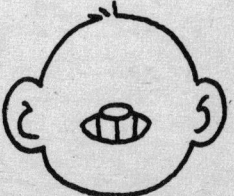

'My dad has his ups and downs.'
   'Does he? Mine just goes around in circles.'

'I assure you he was cut out to be a genius.'
   'It's too bad nobody took the trouble to put
   the pieces together.'

Brenda: 'My dad wanted to be a lawyer
badly.'
Alec: 'Well, he's realized his ambition. He's a
bad lawyer.'

MY SOCK'S LEFT
ME – I'M SO
LONELY!!

'*My sister has learned to speak five languages.*'
  'But she can't say *thank you* in any of them.'

'*My brother is the kind of boy that girls dream of at night.*'
  'That's better than seeing him by daylight.'

Jenny: 'Looks aren't everything.'
Alec: 'In your case they aren't anything.'

'*Do you really think that Jenny is ugly?*'
  'Let's put it this way. When she goes down to the waterfront the tugboats stop whistling.'

'*She has a very sympathetic face.*'
   'Yes, it has everyone's sympathy.'

'*What about her brother? Do you think he's ugly, too?*'
   'What a face! He probably has to sneak up on the mirror to shave.'

'He looks much better without my glasses.'

'*Jenny had a coming-out party.*'
   'With her face, they probably made her go back in again.'

I KNOW!

'I hear when Jenny was born, the doctor took one look at her and slapped her mother!'

'What about Bruce — what do you think of his looks?'
   'I don't mind him looking, it's his face I can't stand!'

'Bruce was a war baby.'
   'I bet. His parents took one look at him and started fighting.'

'He should only go out on Halloween.'
   'Why?'
'It's the only time he can pass as normal.'

'A photographer took his picture but never developed it.'
 'Why?'
'He was afraid to be alone with it in a dark room!'

'Let me sum it up this way: his features don't seem to know the importance of teamwork.'

Caroline: 'I heard that Dilly appeared in a beauty contest and got several offers.'
Alec: 'From plastic surgeons!'

'Mum puts a little oil on her skin at night.'
   'That's why she *slides* out of bed in the
   morning.'

'Mona is no beauty either. At the Christmas
party they're going to hang her and kiss the
mistletoe!'

'She's not really bad-looking.'
   'No, but there's a little blemish between her
   ears — her face!'

Alec: 'Sheila knows how to protect herself
from Peeping Toms.'
Friend: 'How does she do it?'
Alec: 'She leaves the curtains open!'

Friend: 'Everyone says she's like an angel fallen from the sky.'
Alec: 'Too bad she fell on her face.'

'Her skin is nearly as smooth as a prune.'

'She had a face-lift once but it didn't work.'
  'Why not?'
'The derrick broke.'

'Every so often she puts on a mud pack.'
  'Does that help?'
'It improves her looks for a few days, but then the mud falls off!'

'I think she uses gunpowder instead of talcum.'

'What makes you think that?'
'She looks shot to pieces.'

Germaine: 'Mum appears to be getting heavier.'
Alec: 'I've noticed her double chin has become a treble.'

'Dad would like to tickle her under the chin, but he can't decide which one.'

Germaine: 'Do you think she has a big mouth?'
Alec: 'It's so big she can sing a duet all by herself.'

'When she yawns you can't see her ears.'

'Still, she has a pretty head on her shoulders.'
  'Perhaps, but it would be better if there was
  a neck in between.'

'Dad has a Roman nose.'
  'Yes, it roams all over his face.'

'His teeth are like the Ten Commandments.'
  'What do you mean.'
'All broken.'

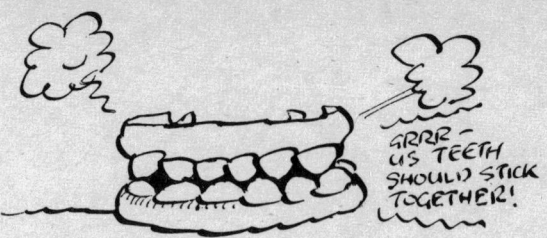

'He goes to the dentist twice a year, once for each tooth!'

'Don't talk badly about dad — he has a heart of gold.'
  'And teeth to match.'

'His teeth are all his own.'
  'You mean he's finished paying for them at last?'

'He's very clean.'
 'Yes, he takes a shower once a month
 whether he thinks he needs it or not.'

Bob: 'Our neighbour is looking rather old.'
Alec: 'Rather? She has so many wrinkles on
her forehead, she has to screw on her hat!'

'And her husband has become so bald, you
can't look at him in a bright light without
sunglasses.'

'Do you think he has big ears?'
 'Big? Why, he can swat flies with them!'

'They say he's short-sighted.'
 'I'll say. He once picked up a snake to kill a stick!'

'His right eye must be fascinating.'
 'Why do you say that?'
'Because his left eye keeps looking at it all the time.'

'It's a pity about his cross-eyes.'
 'Yes, but he can watch a tennis match without moving his head!'

Girlfriend: 'Is it true that carrots improve your sight?'
Alec: 'Have you ever seen a rabbit with glasses?'

Girlfriend: 'Just look: that butterfly used to be a caterpillar.'
Alec: 'I knew it looked familiar!'

Girlfriend: 'Do you realize it takes three sheep just to make one sweater?'
Alec: 'Really? I didn't even know that sheep could knit!'

'Brenda seems quite skinny.'
  'I'd say she has a really *faminine* look!'

THERE HE
IS – AFTER
HIM LADS

'*That sweater doesn't do much for her.*'
   'The way she looks in it, the wool looked
   better on the sheep!'

'She's so skinny, when she's drinking tomato
juice she looks like a thermometer!'

'*Martha looks quite heavy, but she says she's a
light eater.*'
   'She is. As soon as it's light she starts
   eating.'

'*But she eats like a bird.*'
   'Yes, a vulture!'

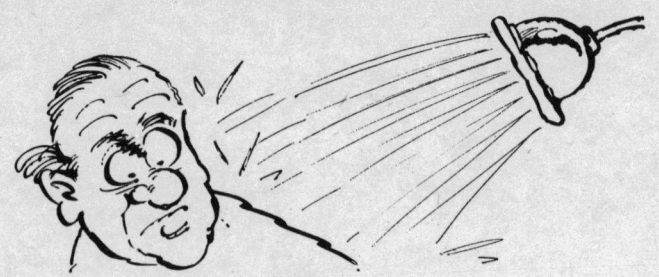

'She's really watching her weight.'
'Watching it go up!'

Gene: 'Diana claims she once had a million-dollar figure.'
Alec: 'Too bad inflation set in.'

'Danny is such a gossip — and he looks very unhappy.'
'That's because he only has one mouth.'

'My dad has put on a lot of weight. His belly's so big, he can now take a shower without getting his feet wet!'

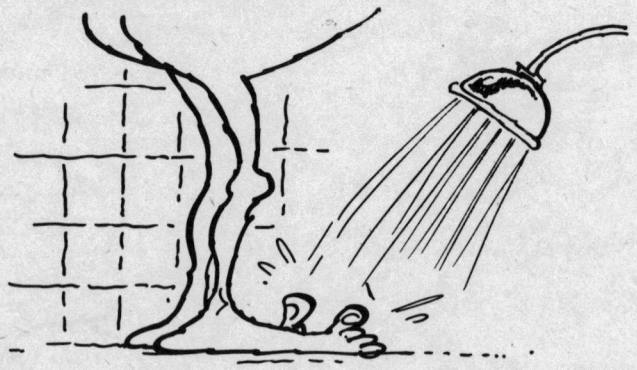

'That man can sit around the table all by himself!'

Father: 'I can't understand where all the grocery money's going to.'
Alec: 'If you really want to know, stand sideways and look in the mirror.'

'Damion likes to have intimate little dinners for two.'
   'Trouble is no one eats them except him.'

'Carol loves Nature.'
   'That's nice of her, considering what Nature did to her!'

Wyatt: 'Carol is so puny-looking.'
Alec: 'I agree. If she ever got married, they won't throw confetti, they'll throw vitamin pills.'

'I wouldn't say she's thin, but she can play hide-and-seek behind a flagpole!'

'For years she's been planning a runaway marriage with her boyfriend. But every time the big day comes, he runs away!'

'Boys don't call her attractive and they don't call her plain. They just don't call her.'

'She was two-thirds married once.'
  'What do you mean?'
'She was there, the minister was there, but the groom didn't show up.'

'Bob has a leaning towards blondes.'
  'I know, but they keep pushing him back.'

'Any girl that goes out with him must appreciate the simpler things in life!'

'His girlfriend returned all his letters.'
  'I bet she marked them *2nd Class Male*.'

'I understand that Bob's father wanted a boy,
and his mother a girl.'
  'With Bob, they can both be satisfied!'

'He's the type that attracts raving beauties.'
  'Escapees from the loony asylum?'

'Bill has a dual personality.'
  'Yeah, Dr Heckle and Mr Snide.'

'People don't like Bill.'
'No. If he ever needs a friend he'll have to buy a dog.'

'Bill hasn't been himself lately.'
'I've noticed the improvement!'

'When he was born the army fired a 21-gun salute.'
'Too bad they missed!'

'Do you think he has many faults?'
'Only two: what he says and what he does!'

'People like him don't grow on trees, they swing from them!'

'Your father is out of this world.'
   'My mum wishes he were.'

'He's a man of many parts.'
   'Yes, but it was a terrible assembly job.'

'He thinks everyone worships the ground he crawled out of!'

'He's the kind of man who could give a headache to an aspirin!'

Alec: 'When my uncle dies they'll bury him face down.'
Henry: 'Why?'
Alec: 'So he'll see where he's going.'

Henry: 'I think a lot of people would go to your uncle's funeral.'
Alec: 'To make sure he's dead?'

'His death notice won't appear in the obituary column, it will be seen in Public Improvements.'

Henry: 'I hear your sister doesn't care for a man's company.'
Alec: 'Not unless he owns it.'

'John took Sue to one of the best restaurants.'
  'So I hear. But he didn't take her in.'

'I hear that your oldest brother married his secretary.'
  'That's right. It was either that or give her a raise.'

IF I STAY HERE – NO ONE WILL EVER FIND ME!

'I'm told he buys her jewellery from a famous millionaire.'
   'True. Woolworth!'

'She wears her wedding ring on the wrong finger.'
   'She probably feels she married the wrong man.'

Henry: 'I hear your dad is a hypochondriac.'
Alec: 'Let's put it this way: he reads the obituary notices to cheer himself up!'

'The way he moans and groans when he gets even a slight cold, you can't decide whether to call a doctor or a drama critic!'

'I hear he's also highly strung.'
 'He's so highly strung I keep telling him to join a circus.'

Ted: 'Morton was born with a silver spoon in his mouth.'
Alec: 'Funny. All the other kids have tongues!'

'He comes up with an answer for every problem.'
 'But it's always wrong!'

'*He's dependable.*'
    'Sure. You can always depend on him to do
    the wrong thing!'

'*I saved for years to buy an unbreakable,
waterproof, shockproof watch.*'
    'How do you like it?'
'*I don't know, I lost it.*'

'Terry has become very stupid. He must have
been practising. You can't be that good at it
by accident!'

'You might say she's a real baboon to society.'

'*To show off his elegant manners, Max holds a teacup with his pinkie sticking out.*'
   'But the teabag is hanging from it!'

'He's the type who keeps an elbow on each arm of his theatre seat.'

'*He never hurts people's feelings.*'
   'Not unintentionally, anyway.'

Martha: 'Why do you say Lillian hasn't got any sense?'
Alec: 'She was having a long discussion with Ted about ropes.'
Martha: 'Why not?'
Alec: 'Ted's father was hanged.'

Dilly: 'Bob is a man with polish.'
Alec: 'Only on his shoes!'

Dilly: 'At the restaurant his table is always reserved.'
Alec: 'Too bad he isn't.'

'He's so dumb, if he walked into a crematorium, he'd probably ask what's cooking.'

'I've always thought of him as a true sportsman.'
'I know what you mean. When he spots an empty seat on a train, he points it out to an old lady, then races her for it!'

'Why does he prefer matches to a lighter?'
'You can't pick your teeth with a lighter.'

'Isn't he a very economical person?'
'Well, he likes to save on soap and water.'

'I think he's a garbage collector. He has a certain air about him.'

'I was told he was bitten by a rattlesnake.'
  'Yes. It was a terrible sight to watch that poor little snake curl up and die!'

Hannah: 'Your brother would never hit a kid when he's down.'
Alec: 'No, he kicks him instead!'

'He always thinks twice before speaking.'
  'Yes, so he can think up something really nasty!'

'When it comes to helping others, he'll stop at nothing!'

Harvey: 'As far as I'm concerned, a friend in need is —'
Alec: 'A friend to steer clear of!'

'You're so cold-blooded, if a mosquito bit you it would die of pneumonia!'

'He reminds me of an accordian player.'
  'Why?'
'Because he plays both ends against the middle.'

THAT'S ME FOLKS

'Why do they call her an after-dinner speaker?'
   'Because every time she speaks to a guy
   she's after a dinner.'

'Why do they call her Angel?'
   'Because she's always harping on things.'

'Why do they call him Bean?'
   'Because all the girls string him along.'

'Why do they call her a Business Woman?'
   'Because her nose is always in everybody's
   business.'

'*Why do they call him Caesar.*'
　'Because he's got a lot of Gaul!'

'*Why do they call him Caterpillar?*'
　'Because he's got where he is by crawling.'

'*Why do they call her Chorus Girl?*'
　'Because she's always kicking.'

'*Why do they call him Cliff?*'
　'Because he's just a big bluff.'

'Why didn't you come to school yesterday?'
   'I was sick — sick of school.'

Father: 'You didn't get a very high mark in your test.'
Alec: 'You don't get a very high salary at work.'

John: 'What's your sister going to be when she grows up?'
Alec: 'An old lady!'

Teacher: 'Classes start at 8.45.'
Alec: 'O.K., but if I'm not here you have my permission to start without me.'

Teacher: 'Where's your homework?'
Alec: 'I made it into a paper plane and someone hijacked it!'

Father: 'I see you got a D for conduct but an A for courtesy. How is that possible?'
Alec: 'Whenever I kick someone I apologize.'

Alec handed in his test paper and said, 'You'll find my answers are a good indication of your ability as a teacher.'

'I thought you said I'd have a choice of greens, but I see only one type of vegetable.'
   'The choice is: take it or leave it!'

Alec: 'Some days I like my teacher.'
Mum: 'When's that?'
Alec: 'When she's sick and has to stay home!'

'Our teacher can do bird imitations.'
   'I know. She watches me like a hawk!'

Alec: 'I'm very tired — I was up till twelve
doing my homework.'
Teacher: 'What time did you begin?'
Alec: 'Eleven fifty-five.'

'*You're pretty dirty, Alec.*'
  'I'm even prettier clean.'

Teacher: 'What do French children say when they've been served a school lunch?'
Alec: 'MERCY!'

Teacher: 'What happens to gold when it's exposed to the air?'
Alec: 'It's probably stolen!'

Teacher: 'Who can name a deadly poison?'
Alec: 'Aviation. One drop and you're dead.'

Alec: 'I have almost 3000 bones in my body.'
Teacher: 'You know that's not possible.'
Alec: 'Yes it is. I had a can of sardines for lunch!'

Teacher: 'Why don't you write more clearly?'
Alec: 'Then you'll realize I can't spell!'

'Why are you so late in school?'
   'I had to say goodbye to my pets.'
'But you're two hours late.'
   'I just got an ant farm!'

GOODBYE GOODBYE GOODBYE GOODBYE GOODBYE GOODBYE

Alec: 'This restaurant must have a very clean kitchen.'
Waiter: 'Thank you. Why do you say that?'
Alec: 'Everything tastes of soap.'

'I didn't come here to be insulted.'
  'Where do you usually go?'

Friend: 'I don't think the photo you took of me does me justice.'
Alec: 'You don't want justice, you want mercy!'

Auntie: 'Do you like my dress. It's over 100 years old.'
Alec: 'Did you make it yourself?'

Friend: 'I've got a head cold. How can I stop it from going to my chest?'
Alec: 'Try tying a knot in your neck.'

Friend: 'That girl looks like Helen Green.'
Alec: 'She looks even worse in red!'

Dora: 'Some boys think I'm pretty and some think I'm ugly. What do you think?'
Alec: 'A bit of both — pretty ugly!'

'Why do you keep telling everyone I'm an idiot?'
    'Surely you're not trying to keep it secret?'

'In the park I was surrounded by lions.'
  'Lions in the park?'
'That's right, dandelions.'

Father: 'Did you get my golf gear?'
Alec: 'Yes, here's your map, compass, emergency rations . . .'

Friend: 'Your dad's a fanatical golfer.'
Alec: 'Yes. You might say, he's a real crack putt!'

Friend: 'Your dad got a birdie on the 4th?'
Alec: 'Yes, a poor little sparrow . . .'

BOY- THIS TASTES BETTER THAN BONES

Girlfriend: 'What's a caddie?'
Alec: 'Someone who follows his work schedule to a tee!'

Golfer: 'You must be the worst caddie in the world.'
Alec (as caddy): 'I doubt that, sir, it would be too much of a coincidence!'

Golfer: 'I'd move heaven and earth to break 100.'
Alec: 'Concentrate on heaven — you've already moved enough earth!'

Golfer: 'Do you like my game?'
Alec: 'Not bad, but I still prefer golf!'

Girlfriend: 'Will you love me when I'm old and ugly?'
Alec: 'Of course I do!'

Alec: 'I'm the most advanced kid in the class.'
Mum: 'Really?'
Alec: 'Yes, I sit at the front.'

Friend: 'What does your father do?'
Alec: 'He's a government artist.'
Friend: 'What does he draw?'
Alec: 'The dole!'

Sister: 'For my birthday I'd like a dress to match the colour of my eyes.'
Alec: 'Where can I buy a bloodshot dress?'

Alec: 'You look like a real dishy Italian.'
Wanda: 'Like Sophia Loren?'
Alec: 'No, spaghetti.'

Sister: 'There's a man at the door collecting for old people.'
Alec: 'Let's give him Granny!'

Wanda: 'Do you think it will rain today?'
Alec: 'It all depends on the weather.'

Alec: 'I can't leave you.'
Girlfriend: 'Do you love me so much?'
Alec: 'Its not that. You're standing on my feet.'

Girlfriend: 'I'm the teacher's pet.'
Alec: 'Can't she afford a cat?'

Friend: 'Every time I feel down in the dumps I buy myself a new suit.'
Alec: 'So *that's* where you get your clothes!'

Friend: 'My girlfriend's really smart. She has brains enough for two.'
Alec: 'Sounds like the right girl for you.'

Teacher: 'If you had to multiply 327 by 829, what would you get?'
Alec: 'The wrong answer.'

Father: 'I hope you're not talking in class any more?'
Alec: 'Not any more, just about the same amount!'

Teacher: 'I'd like to go one whole day without having to scold you.'
Alec: 'Well, you have my permission.'

Teacher: 'I take great pleasure in giving you 90 in maths.'
Alec: 'Why don't you let your hair down. Enjoy yourself. Give me 100!'

Teacher: 'If you had five chocolate bars and your friend asked for one of them, how many would you have left?'
Alec: 'Five.'

Teacher: 'How do you make sugar cubes?'
Alec: 'From square sugar beet.'

George: 'Nancy and Mike make a perfect pair, don't you think?'
Alec: 'Yes. He's a pill and she's a headache!'

George: 'Roger will never be a leader of men.'
Alec: 'I agree — but he's a great follower of women!'

'Nancy's father is a blacksmith.'
  'Is that why she's forging ahead?'

'Betty's father is a chimneysweep.'
  'Is that why he wears a soot?'

'Elinor's mother is a clergyman.'
  'And you certainly can't put anything pastor.'

'Wanda's mother is a doctor.'
  'Boy! Can she operate!'

'Sheila's only a draftsman's daughter, but she sure knows where to draw the line.'

'Freda's mother is a dressmaker.'
  'And Freda knows how to keep the fellows on pins and needles.'

'Carol's an electrician's daughter.'
  'She certainly has good connections.'

REST PERIOD

CONSTABLE CLENCH NEVER RESTS

'Harry's the son of a fireman.'
'Yes. Poor old Harry. He's going to blazes!'

'Ned is the son of a fisherman.'
'All the girls seem to swallow his line.'

'John's mother is an optician.'
'Is that why John keeps making a spectacle of himself?'

'Monica is a postman's daughter. She knows her males.'

George: 'Randy has a mechanical mind.'
Alec: 'But some of the screws are loose.'

'When he was a baby we called him our little acorn. Now he's grown up, he's a big nut!'

'When Johnny goes to a zoo he needs two tickets.'
   'Why?'
'One to get in and one to get out.'

Ben: 'Jack flies off the handle a lot!'
Alec: 'No wonder. He has a screw loose!'

'In one way Jack is fortunate. He could go out of his mind but no one would know the difference!'

'I hear Gary is girl crazy.'
'Yes, girls won't go out with him, that's why he's crazy!'

Friend: 'I think Josephine has a big mouth.'
Alec: 'Put it this way. She eats bananas sideways!'

'And Belinda thinks she's a great entertainer.'
  'That's a laugh, she couldn't entertain a doubt!'

'She needs better gags.'
  'Yes, to stop her opening her mouth.'

'She has a waterproof voice.'
  'What do you mean?'
'It can't be drowned out.'

'Do you think her success has gone to her head?'
  'Well, it's certainly gone to her mouth!'

'She said she would only marry a guy who could take a joke.'
   'That's the only kind who would take her!'

'She is so particular she won't even eat a hot dog unless it's been certified by the Kennel Club!'

'Jake says he can trace his family tree way back.'
   'Yeah, back to the time he lived in it!'

'His family are real snobs. They have monogrammed tea bags!'

'A few minutes with Jake and I feel like jumping for joy.'
    'I feel like jumping off the roof.'

'He's a person who's going places.'
    'The sooner the better!'

'He holds people openmouthed with his conversation.'
    'Of course, they can't stop yawning.'

'He's just what the doctor ordered. A real pill!'

'He's a bit dull till you get to know him. After that he's a real bore!'

Ginger: 'They say that Wendy's stories always have a happy ending.'
Alec: 'Well, everyone is happy when they end!'

'George is good for people's health. When they see him coming they take a long walk!'

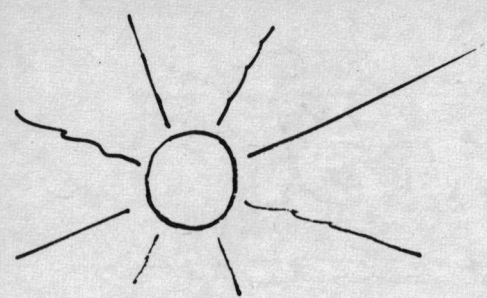

'*But George is a man of few words.*'
   'That's right, but he keeps repeating them!'

'No one can equal him for squeezing a minimum of thought into a maximum of verbiage!'

'As soon as he opens his mouth he bites his toe!'

'He's like a summer cold.'
  'What do you mean?'
'You can't get rid of him!'

'He's a boring fellow but he does have occasional flashes of silence.'

'It's not that he doesn't know how to say nothing, he just doesn't know when!'

Henry: 'Linda is a fast speaker.'
Alec: 'I'll say! She can speak 120 words a minute, with gusts up to 200!'

'I hear she always has to have the last word.'
 'That wouldn't be so bad if she ever reached it.'

'From the day they were married her husband hasn't been on speaking terms with her, only on listening terms!'

'The only time she listens to him is when he talks in his sleep.'

'Before Linda got married, her chin was her best feature.'
 'Things have improved. Now it's a double feature!'

---

* THIS IS A GREAT MOMENT FOR ALL READERS OF THIS BOOK. SMART ALEXANDER HAS HOOFED OFF OUT OF IT AND WON'T APPEAR UNTIL A LATER VOLUME!

READERS – REJOICE !!

Albert: 'I got a cute poodle for my girlfriend.'
Alec: 'I wish I could make a trade like that!'

'My girlfriend gave me a present that made my eyes pop out, a shirt with a collar two sizes too small.'

'Andrew took my sister for better or for worse, but he didn't mean *that* much worse.'

'When they got married my sister took Andrew for better of worse, and when they got divorced she took him for everything!'

'She loved him for what he was — sick and wealthy!'

Sister: 'I've lost my warm feelings for Andrew.'
Alec: 'You'll soon get them back when he buys you a fur coat!'

'My sister wanted to marry a man clever enough to make a lot of money — and dumb enough to spend it all on her!'

'When he proposed, he declared he'd go through anything for my sister. So far he's only gone through her bank account!'

'Her boyfriend told her he'd lost all his money.'
    'What did she say?'
'I'll miss you, honey!'

'Gary has provided himself with a modern kitchen.'
    'Now he's looking for an old-fashioned girl.'

'When I'm near death I'll ask Sally to cook my last meal.'
    'Why?'
'I'll feel more like dying!'

'She's burned so much bread, her toaster has been declared a fire hazard.'

'Sally told me she'd cook dinner and asked what I would like. I told her a life-insurance policy!'

'She doesn't know much about cooking, but she can bring her husband to the boiling point!'

George: 'Before she was married your sister turned her husband's head with her charms.'
Alec: 'Now she turns his stomach with her cooking!'

'I hear there are always grounds in her coffee.'
  'There's enough grounds for a divorce!'

'Some people can cook but don't.'
  'My sister can't cook but does.'

'Does she keep a messy home?'
  'Let's put it this way, when the toast pops
  out of the toaster, it takes an hour to find
  it!'

'The air pollution is terrible. Even the sun
gives indirect lighting.'

'The air is so bad that artificial respiration is better than the real thing!'

'I understand the city will soon deal with air pollution.'
    'As soon as it sees its way clear!'

'Thomas Edison once said that genius is 1% inspiration and 99% perspiration.'
    'I hate to think of anyone that sweaty handling electricity!'

'My father goes to church regularly.'
    'So I hear. Once a year, no matter how bad the weather.'

Jay: 'Your dad is really bald.'
Alec: 'He thinks of himself as simply having a wide parting!'

Jay: 'Did you know that camping attracts 25 million a year?'
Alec: 'Are you talking about people or mosquitoes?'

Jason: 'There's Harriet. Her mother almost lost her as a child.'
Alec: 'She probably didn't take her far enough into the woods!'

Shopkeeper: 'So you want a job? Do you ever tell lies?'
Alec: 'No, but I can learn!'

Passer-by: 'You shouldn't hit a boy when he's down.'
Alec: 'What do you think I got him down for?'

Father: 'Who gave you that black eye?'
Alec: 'Nobody gave it to me, I had to fight for it!'

Fred: 'Do you come from a tough neighbourhood?'
Alec: 'It's so tough that anybody who still has his own teeth is considered a sissy!'

'Earlier today a body was discovered with ten bullet holes, a dozen stab wounds and a rope around the neck. The police suspect foul play!'

Judge: 'Guilty or not guilty?'
Alec: 'Any other choices?'

Judge: 'This man's wallet was deep in his inside pocket. How did you manage to get it out?'
Alec: 'Well, your Honour. I usually charge ten pounds a lesson.'

Judge: 'Guilty or not guilty?'
Alec: 'I'll let you know after I've heard the evidence.'

Judge: 'When were you born?'
Alec: 'Why do you want to know? Do you want to send me a birthday present?'

Judge: 'This is the tenth time you've appeared in court. I fine you 100 pounds.'
Alec: 'Don't I get a discount for being a good customer?'

Auntie: 'Are you a good boy?'
Alec: 'No, I'm the kind of kid my mother doesn't want me to play with!'

THE SOCKS RUN - AWAY WITH THE TEETH - SMART-Y PANTS ALEC'S GONE - EVEN MY FLEAS HAVE LEFT!

Neighbour: 'Andrea is a liar, a cheat and a thief.'
Alec: 'She's improving!'

Ken: 'Has your father ever raised his hand to you?'
Alec: 'Only in self-defence!'

Ken: 'Did you come from a tough neighbourhood?'
Alec: 'Tough? The teachers didn't give us marks, just bruises!'

Auntie: 'Do you ever lie?'
Alec: 'Let's just say my memory exaggerates!'

Father: 'Why don't you play cards with Billy any more?'
Alec: 'Would you play cards with someone who cheats?'
Father: 'No.'
Alec: 'Neither will Billy.'

'A convict has escaped from Parkhurst by helicopter. The police have set up road blocks on all the main highways.'

Henry: 'A man has been sentenced to 200 years in prison.'
Alec: 'He's lucky he didn't get life!'

Alec: 'If I was a hangman I'd be kind-hearted.'
Friend: 'How so?'
Alec: 'I'd always ask the condemned man if the noose was too tight!'

THANKS SPENCER-BABY!

Teacher: 'I wish you'd pay a little attention.'
Alec: 'I'm paying as little as possible!'

Teacher: 'Don't whistle while you're studying.'
Alec: 'I'm not studying, just whistling.'

Teacher: 'I'm expelling you from class!'
Alec: 'No you're not — I resign!'

Teacher: 'If I had ten flies on my desk and I swatted one, how many would be left?'
Alec: 'One — the dead one!'

Mother: 'Do you want to come?'
Alec: 'No thanks, I don't want to mangle with the crowds!'

Alec: 'I know how to get extra Christmas presents.'
Friend: 'How?'
Alec: 'I'm putting up a *stretch* sock!'

Janet: 'Little Paulie comes from a wealthy family.'
Alec: 'Wealthy! His father gave him a chauffeur-driven kiddie-car for Christmas!'

Mother: 'How many times do I have to tell you to stay away from the Christmas pudding?'
Alec: 'Never again, Mum, I just finished it.'

Father: 'What did I say I'd do to you if you ate your mother's Christmas pudding?'
Alec: 'Gee Dad, my memory's as bad as yours. I can't remember either!'

Girlfriend: 'Just think, next week is Christmas, and a year ago I didn't even know you.'
Alec: 'Never mind about our past, think about my present.'

Mum: 'Here's three bags of Christmas sweets for you and your sister.'
Alec: 'It's difficult to divide three, so I'll keep one and divide the other two!'

Alec: 'I wish you'd sing only Christmas carols.'
Sister: 'Why?'
Alec: 'Then I'd only have to listen to you once a year!'

Dottie: 'Look what Chris gave me for Christmas, a mink stole.'
Alec: 'I'm not sure it's mink, but I'm certain it's *stole*!'

Alec: 'You have to believe in Father Christmas.'
Brother: 'Why?'
Alec: 'Otherwise, we're all being good for no reason!'

Friend: 'I hear your mum is hoping for diamonds for Christmas.'
Alec: 'Knowing my dad, it'll more likely be spades or club.'

Henry: 'I'm going to give my dad a cordless shaver for Christmas.'
Alec: 'Yeah, coarse sandpaper.'

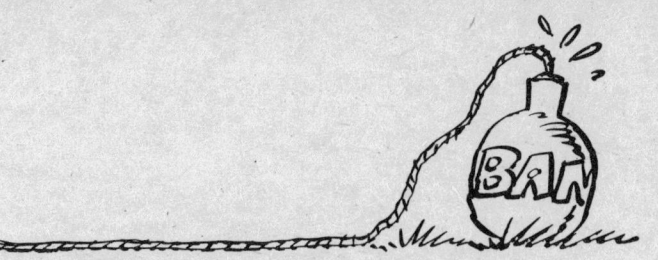

Alec: 'I'm going to give you a teapot for Christmas.'
Mum: 'But I already have a teapot.'
Alec: 'No you don't, I just dropped it!'

Alec walked into a candy shop and asked the salesman to wrap up a 5p piece of bubble gum.
   'A surprise for your little sister for Christmas?'
   'It certainly will be. She thinks I'm giving her a big doll.'

Mum: 'I want to give your father something up-to-date and striking for Christmas. Any suggestions?'
Alec: 'How about a quartz alarm clock?'

Mum: 'And what would you like?'
Alec: 'A train set, model plane, bicycle, and an end to my violin lessons!'

Teacher: 'If your father earned 600 pounds a week and gave your mother half, what would she have?'
Alec: 'Heart failure!'

Alec: 'I went to the zoo on Saturday.'
Teacher: 'Really? I was there also.'
Alec: 'Funny, I looked in all the cages but didn't see you!'

Headmaster: 'From today there will be no more physical punishment in this school.'
Alec: 'I guess that means no more school dinners!'

Mother: 'Do you know a boy named Harry Graves?'
Alec: 'Yes, he sleeps next to me in history.'

FOOT OF CONSTABLE OF OLD ENGLAND!

Teacher: 'Did you know Christopher Columbus discovered America?'
Alec: 'I didn't even know it was lost!'

Alec told his father: 'Remember you promised me ten pounds if I passed my maths. Well, I've got great news. You've just saved ten pounds!'

Mother: 'What does this F mean on your report?'
Alec: 'Fantastic!'

'My mum suffers from a neurosis, every time she sees my report she faints!'

'Jerry's father looks pretty old.'
  'That's an understatement. When he was a boy history was probably called Current Events!'

Teacher: 'Where did Hitler keep his armies?'
Alec: 'Up his sleevies!'

Teacher: 'Did your father help you with your homework?'
Alec: 'No, I got it wrong all by myself!'

Father: 'Why do you call your teacher "Treasure"?'
Alec: 'Because I wonder where she was dug up!'

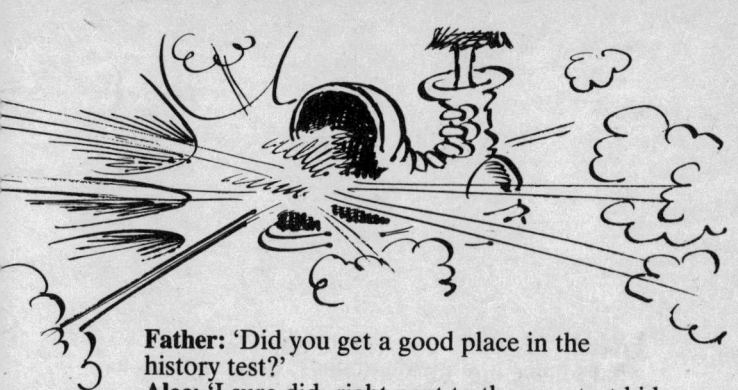

Father: 'Did you get a good place in the history test?'
Alec: 'I sure did, right next to the smartest kid in class!'

Alec: 'I've got a part in the school Christmas play.'
Mother: 'What are you going to play?'
Alec: 'A part best suited to me, one of the three wise guys!'

Mother: 'I'm going Christmas shopping, but I dread the crowds.'
Alec: 'Yeah, they're full of brotherly shove!'

Friend: 'My dad's very rich, I don't know what to give him for Christmas. What do you give to a man who has everything?'
Alec: 'A burglar alarm?'

Friend: 'Last year mum served a special turkey for Christmas and everyone was tickled.'
Alec: 'I guess she forgot to remove the feathers!'

Friend: 'I'm going to have a dog for Christmas.'
Alec: 'Really? We're going to have a turkey as usual!'

Department Store Santa Claus: 'And what would you like for Christmas?'
Alec: 'I wrote you last week, you idiot. I knew you'd forget!'

Friend: 'What do you mean Yuletide Greetings?'
Alec: 'Lend me ten pounds and you'll tide me over till Christmas!'

Alec told his friend, 'My father's always more interested in my presents than I am. What I'd like for Christmas is something to separate the men from the toys!'

Tony: 'My mum says that cleanliness is next to godliness.'
Alec: 'With my little sister it's next to impossible.'

Big sister: 'We ought to all help in cleaning up the environment.'
Alec: 'I agree. You could start with your room.'

'My sister's dressing gown gets more dirty from the inside than outside!'

Jane: 'I hear that your two sisters stick together.'
Alec: 'If you took a bath as little as they do, you'd be a little gummy too!'

'Some kids train to be doctors or lawyers when they grow up. My sister's training to be a swamp.'

FLY PAST

Jane: 'But she's such a sweet girl! Everyone loves her!'
Alec: 'Sure, 10,000 flies can't be wrong!'

'Mum has to wash her with oven-cleaner!'

'Her room is so dirty the cockroaches have left!'

Alec: 'I'm going to give my girlfriend an old-time washing machine for her birthday.'
Friend: 'What's that?'
Alec: 'A flat stone!'

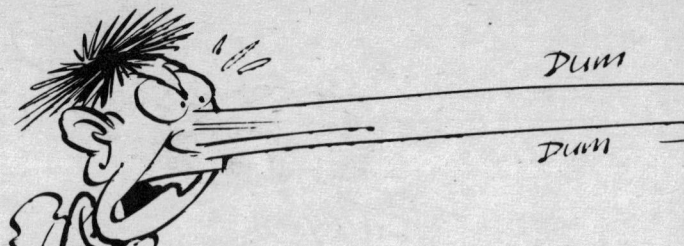

Alec: 'My big brother took eight years to finish college. He's a D.D.'
Friend: 'A doctor of divinity?'
Alec: 'No, a dum-dum!'

'I don't want to say he's stupid, but when he had to fill out a questionnaire he was stumped on the first line. It said "Name?" '

Friend: 'People are using a lot of recycled paper these days.'
Alec: 'I'll get excited about recycled paper when they can make trees out of it!'

Friend: 'My mother is an authority on Ancient Greece.'
Alec: 'You mean she never cleans the oven!'

'My mum loves to eat out. We've lived in our new flat for over a year, and she still doesn't know where the kitchen is!'

'She's a modern cook. Her favourite recipe is heat and serve!'

Alec: 'We have an "Autumn Leaves" fridge.'
Friend: 'What's that?'
Alec: 'Everything turns brown.'

'The bread in our house comes in three types — white, brown, and mouldy!'

Friend: 'Crime on the streets is on the increase.'
Alec: 'I'll say. It's so bad that when Clark Kent goes into a phone booth, he's afraid to come out!'

'It's so bad the muggers will soon be calling for help!'

Alec: 'Is it true the human race springs from dust?'
Friend: 'That's what I'm told.'
Alec: 'Well, under my sister's bed is the birth of a nation!'

'Sam's new disc is a record-breaker.'
  'So I hear. Every time someone listens to it they break it!'

'There are a lot of fans at his show.'
  'They probably can't afford air-conditioning!'

'When he puts on a show there's never a dull moment. The dullness lasts for hours unbroken!'

'I'd like to say he's a wonderful singer. I'd like to . . . but I never lie.'

Gerald: 'What exactly is a cashew?'
Alec: 'I think of it as a peanut with back trouble!'

Friend: 'The value of gold is increasing.'
Alec: 'If it keeps going up, dentists will be mugging their patients!'

Friend: 'I hear all the colleges are faced with a dope problem.'
Alec: 'Yes. Take a look at the grades!'

'*A hamburger chain paid an employee 100 pounds for his suggestion of putting more meat in the hamburgers.*'
   'That must have been his severance pay!'

'My mum went to one of those health farms to take off weight. She came back 100 pounds lighter, but she hadn't lost any weight!'

Father: 'The first thing you should do with a garden is turn it over.'
Alec: 'If I were you, I'd turn it over to someone who knows what they're doing!'

Father: 'Plants grow faster if you talk to them.'
Alec: 'But I don't know how to speak Geranium!'

John: 'Your garden looks like heaven.'
Alec: 'Yeah, but the gardener looks like hell.'

John: 'What's the secret of a green thumb?'
Alec: 'It is not so much a green thumb. You have to have brown knees!'

John: 'What's nice about a garden is that everyday you can have something freshly cut.'
Alec: 'Somedays, flowers, other days fingers!'

John: 'I hear Pauline is pretty mean.'
Alec: 'That's right. Her idea of a manicure is to bite her nails!'

John: 'They say she cooks health food.'
Alec: 'They say it because you have to be in perfect health to eat it and survive.'

'My folks go to organic restaurants, where they add nothing to the food.'
   'No, but they add a bit to the price!'

'John, you'd make a great parole officer. You never let anyone finish a sentence.'

'Mary talks like a Xerox machine.'
   'What do you mean?'
'She keeps repeating herself!'

'She has a very sharp tongue.'
  'Yeah, she uses it for slicing tomatoes!'

'We've just moved into a new flat. It comes with faucet-type plumbing.'
  'What is that?'
'Whenever you want something to work you have to faucet!'

Alec: 'My mum is a little over the top when it comes to keeping things clean.'
Friend: 'Why do you say that?'
Alec: 'Twice a week she vacuums the lawn!'

Friend: 'My father says there's no authority in the home.'
Alec: 'My father doesn't feel that way. He knows whatever I say, goes!'

John: 'Just listen to that folk singer singing the "Hard-up" blues.'
Alec: 'Yeah, on his £20,000 sound system.'

John: 'My parents are going to buy a water bed.'
Alec: 'They'd better cut their toenails too!'

Alec: 'You need glasses.'
Father: 'Why do you say that?'
Alec: 'There's newsprint on the tip of your nose!'

Alec: 'My mum is too efficient.'
Friend: 'What do you mean?'
Alec: 'Whenever she goes on a two-week diet, she finishes it in three days!'

Tim: 'I think Sara has a wonderful personality.'
Alec: 'I agree. She probably gets thank-you notes from muggers!'

'Is she ugly?'
  'Well, when a mosquito bites her, it shuts its eyes.'

Sister: 'What's the meaning of industrial waste?'
Alec: 'That's when you have three million unemployed!'

Jerry: 'The post office keeps putting up the price of postage.'
Alec: 'I have an idea. Why not use smaller stamps?'

Alec: 'Dad is suffering from a low-grade infection.'
Friend: 'How did he get it?'
Alec: 'Every time he sees my report card he gets sick!'

Alec: 'Dad can't bear to see mum shovelling snow.'
Friend: 'What does he do about it?'
Alec: 'He draws the curtains.'

Friend: 'I went away to a camp for kids last summer. We really had to rough it.'
Alec: 'What does that mean — only black & white TV?'

Friend: 'When I went on holiday I changed my ideas, my habits, my routines . . .'
Alec: 'Did you ever change your underwear?'

Friend: 'I just bought a tortoise.'
Alec: 'The trouble with tortoises is you can't tell when they're dead!'

Alec: 'Our house got flooded in the rain.'
Friend: 'Where is your house?'
Alec: 'Around the corner. You can't miss it, it's the one with the periscope on the roof.'

'Thousands of people had a lucky escape at the rock concert. The band never turned up!'

Friend: 'It's a great little band.'
Alec: 'Yes, four boys with hearts of gold, wills of steel — and ears of tin!'

'They are improving. Now you can tell when they're tuning up!'

Friend: 'I'm trying to form a four-piece band.'
Alec: 'Too bad you only know three pieces!'

'You keep playing that guitar out of tune.'
   'It's not my fault. The electricity is flat!'

'Now I'm going to give you my impression of my friend singing. First, I hit my thumb with a hammer!'

Friend: 'Look, this review says the rock concert we attended was wonderful, and that everyone loved it.'
Alec: 'Really? I had no idea I enjoyed it that much!'

'When I hear that band, I say to myself, if Vincent Van Gogh were alive he'd probably cut off *both* ears!'

Friend: 'Do you ever listen to contemporary rock groups?'
Alec: 'Occasionally — just to remind myself of how much I appreciate the Beatles!'

Mum: 'Maybe you can give your sister a rock album for Christmas.'
Alec: 'Not a chance. She's got too many already!'
Mum: 'But she's only got one.'
Alec: 'That's right. One too many.'

'Anyone who thinks that practice makes perfect should listen to my neigbour's drum lessons!'

Father: 'That guitar is driving me mad!'
Alec: 'But Dad, I don't think you need driving.'

Friend: 'Guitars are harmless.'
Alec: 'Yes, as long as people would only leave them alone!'

Alec: 'I've stopped playing guitar.'
Sister: 'Why?'
Alec: 'Dad removed a few bits and I'm tired of practising without strings!'

Little sister: 'What's classical music?'
Alec: 'Any music without an electric guitar!'

'My friend's an atheist. He doesn't believe in Elvis Presley!'

'I'm developing a new record for people who hate rock music. It spins at 156 rpm. It doesn't sound any better, but it's over quicker!'

AAAAAA.

NOPE! HE'S ALIVE OK!

'I hear your sister has a great collection of rock records.'
    'Yes, and they've proved very educational. Every time she plays one I go into my room and read a book!'

Sister: 'What's jazz?'
Alec: 'The kind of music in which it doesn't matter what notes you play.'

Friend: 'Some rock musicians look terrible.'
Alec: 'True. I saw one the other night with a dirty shirt, no shoes, long smelly hair and a rough beard — but she sounded great!'

MAAAAAAARRGG

Friend: 'How can those rock musicians afford all that sound equipment they carry?'
Alec: 'Well, just think of all the money they've saved on music lessons!'

Friend: 'I hear your sister has a large collection of jazz records.'
Alec: 'Yes, and the thing I detest most about it is that they're all unbreakable albums!'

Friend: 'The rock concert started at eight sharp.'
Alec: 'And it ended at ten dull.'

Friend: 'Listen to this. Isn't that a sad song?'
Alec: 'Pitiful, I'd say!'

Friend: 'What did you think of her singing?'
Alec: 'It reminded me that my dad's car needs a tuneup!'

Friend: 'Do you think the pollution is really bad?'
Alec: 'Are you kidding? Nowadays it's dangerous to open the window and let the fresh air in!'

'It's a wonderful city. I love to wake up in the morning and hear the birds coughing!'

Larry: 'What do you want to be when you grow up?'
Alec: 'With all this pollution I'll be happy to be alive!'

Alec: 'I'm developing a great new product.'
Friend: 'What?'
Alec: 'A mouthwash for people who drink the water!'

Little sister: 'What exactly is pollution?'
Alec: 'It's contamination of Mother Nature by human nature.'

'Look at all this rubbish.'
    'Yeah, it's a great social problem — grime in the streets!'

Father: 'There's an energy crisis in our office.'
Alec: 'You mean your boss is expecting you to show some!'

Little sister: 'What's gossip?'
Alec: 'Ear pollution.'

Little sister: 'What's dandruff?'
Alec: 'Hair pollution.'

He feels the only way we're going to make it
through the winter is to use fuels that increase
pollution. Alec says the choice is ours:
wheezing or freezing!

Alec: 'Air pollution makes people very polite.'
Friend: 'How so?'
Alec: 'Today I saw a man tip his hat three
times, once to a lady, and twice to knock the
soot off!'

Alec: 'My cousin died of lead poisoning.'
Friend: 'How did that happen?'
Alec: 'Someone shot him!'

Alec: 'The Noise Abatement Society should
send my sister a button.'
Friend: 'Why?'
Alec: 'For her lip!'

Little brother: 'What's an environmentalist?'
Alec: 'Someone worried about the effluence of affluence.'

Friend: 'Your mother should give up smoking.'
Alec: 'I don't know. It's probably safer than breathing!'

Alec: 'Remember the good old days?'
Friend: 'When?'
Alec: 'When if you had a picnic the black specks on your food were pepper!'

'Alec says he knows why some birds sleep on one foot. They're using the other one to hold their nose!'

Doctor: 'Your dad will be all right. All he needs is clean fresh air.'
Alec: 'In that case we'll have to move to another planet!'

Alec: 'The smog is getting worse.'
Friend: 'Why do you say that?'
Alec: 'This morning I thought I saw a thrush. Then I realized it was a sparrow holding its breath!'

Alec wants to know how can a lake stay clean if there are no toilets for the fish.

Alec: 'Did you hear about the man who jumped off Tower Bridge?'
Friend: 'What happened?'
Alec: 'He committed sewercide!'

'You want to know what the water in the Thames is like? Wait a minute, I'll get you a slice!'

'Alec says the Red Sea is connected to the Mediterranean by the Sewage Canal!'

Alec: 'Did you hear about the fireman who was treated for smoke inhalation?'
Friend: 'No.'
Alec: 'It was his day off!'

'I shot an arrow into the air and — it stuck!'

Alec: 'I'm afraid to play outside.'
Friend: 'Why?'
Alec: 'I'll get my lungs dirty!'

Little sister: 'What are organic gardeners?'
Alec: 'People who till it like it is!'

Alec says, 'Keep London tidy. Eat a pigeon a day!'

The Good Old Days — when radioactivity meant listening to the wireless!'

'In a nuclear war, all people are cremated equal.'

Little sister: 'What's a desert?'
Alec: 'A region that needs a flood transfusion!'

Alec says that autumn is the time of year when leaves slowly turn from green to brown to gold to litter!

'Go jogging, and die healthier!'

Friend: 'I hear you live on the 15th floor of a high-rise block. Do you have a good view?'
Alec: 'Yes, on a clear day you can see the ground!'

Ashes to ashes
Dust to dust
If cigarettes don't get you
The atmosphere must!

Father: 'The cost of airline tickets is astronomical.'
Alec: 'Don't complain. You're only charged what's fare!'

Alec hates flying. He says you can never walk out of a dull movie!

I'M OFF FANS—SEE YOU IN MY NEXT BOOK!

Alec: 'My dad was on an airliner which had engine trouble.'
Friend: 'What did he do?'
Alec: 'He offered to get out and push.'

'What made you nervous about the flight?'
  'Seeing the pilot's instrument panel, and realizing it was in braille!'

Alec thinks that air sickness is one of the few things that can make you look like your passport photo!

Alec is so terrified of flying, he feels sick just licking an airmail stamp!

Alec is developing a new parachute. It opens on impact!

Alec: 'We're going to Minorca.'
Friend: 'Flying?'
Alec: 'No, we're going by plane.'

Friend: 'Thanks to airmail, letters go from London to New York in one day.'
Alec: 'Especially letters addressed to Chicago!'

Little sister: 'How do you become a pilot?'
Alec: 'You start at the bottom and work your way up!'

Alec says a pilot's wife is the only woman who loves to see her husband down and out!

Father: 'Why do you insist on flying first class?'
Alec: 'You meet a better class of hijacker!'

Alex gets so airsick, he says the airline slogan, 'Up, Up and Away!' refers to his lunch.

'*Wanda is a naturally talented cello player.*'
  'I can tell that by her bow legs!'

Alex says that to play the harp you need a lot of pluck.

'*What's a tuba?*'
  'It comes between a oneba and a threeba!'

'*A tuba is an instrument.*'
  'Not when it's a tuba toothpaste!'

Alec says that Harry should be an organist because he has so many pipe dreams!

Burt: 'Someone stole our upright piano.'
Alec: 'That's downright annoying.'

Burt: 'I hear he has a terrific technique on the piano.'
Alec: 'Yes, he can play the minute waltz in 55 seconds!'

Burt: 'What do you have to know to play cymbals in an orchestra?'
Alec: 'Nothing, just when!'

'What was the first thing you learned after you got a drum for your birthday?'
  'I learned that I'll never get another one again!'

'What's a brass band?'
  'An orchestra with no strings attached.'

'Listen to that chamber music on the radio.'
  'It sounds like torture chamber music!'